Story-Selling for the Modern MLM Leader

10 Core Stories That Do the Heavy Lifting for You

by Sydney Brown

Ready to Get to Work?

Free Gift Membership!

Congratulations on your decision to take this journey into storytelling. This book is a full reference guide and alone, it could help you change the world. But, I realized many people struggled to find people to practice their stories with.

I'm excited to announce the startup of the BS Community! And I'd like to invite you to join me and my storytelling friends as we learn, grow, practice without judgment, and continue on this great journey of life.

You are formally invited to join us in the Just BS Community. Oh, come on now! What did you think that stood for?

We're a growing community of Basic (or Badass, you decide) Storytellers.

Some stick to *telling* their stories, and some *write* them. Most also have side gigs and are there to practice skills in a safe space and to make friends without the pressure of having to be perfect because we all are A-Okay with being authentic!

The Community membership is free, and if you enter the group through the URL below, you will be granted a free $29 evaluation of your Origin or Signature story (up to 10 minutes) with the purchase of this book. Either way, we're excited to see you and hear your stories!

We hope to see you there! → SellingWithYourStory.com

ISBN: 978-1-959948-32-2
Printed in the United States
Published by TLM Publishing House, New Albany, IN.

Dedication

To the ones who kept showing up when it would've been easier to walk away.

To the quiet builders, the late-night thinkers, the bold beginners, and the tired-but-still-trying.

To every person who hit "publish" with shaky hands, or spoke with a quivered voice, then followed up with a racing heart, or wondered if their story was even worth telling.

This is for you.

For those who've been overlooked, underestimated, or told to tone it down.

For those who've tried and failed and tried again.

For those still chasing a life that feels aligned, one story at a time.

You are not too late.

You are not alone.

And your voice still matters.

This book was written with you in mind.

Keep telling your story. That's how movements start, and how leaders are made.

Contents

Introduction

If you're holding this book, I already know something about you. You're ready to lead, but not with hype. You're ready to grow, but not by faking it. And most of all, you're ready to do this in a way that actually feels good. Real. Sustainable. Duplicatable.

Welcome to *Story-Selling for the Modern MLM Leader*. This isn't just another book about selling. It's a book about storytelling...strategic storytelling that fuels income, impact, and influence in the network marketing world without turning you into a clone, a spam bot, or a "hey girl" message machine.

Why stories? Because stories are what stick. They're how people make decisions, build trust, and remember what matters. Stories bridge the gap between strangers and supporters, browsers and buyers, team members and true believers.

But most network marketers are never taught which stories to tell, or how to tell them. They end up overwhelmed, overthinking, and oversharing... or worse, staying silent because they just don't know where to start.

That changes now.

Inside this book, we're getting laser-focused on the **10 essential stories** every network marketer needs to be able to tell. These aren't just fluffy anecdotes. They're conversion tools. Confidence builders. Connection starters. And best of all, they're teachable, trainable, and totally duplicable.

This is the stuff you pass down to your team. The stuff you master once and reuse endlessly. The stories that let people feel something *real* about your message and say, "I get it, and I want in."

Here's what you can expect:

- A clear framework for each of the 10 stories
- Prompts to help you craft your own version without getting stuck
- Buyer personality insights so you know which stories speak to whom
- Real-life examples and story templates to model
- A repeatable system you can plug into your business and team trainings

You'll also get my honest take... no fluff, no guru nonsense. Just the storytelling strategies I use to grow my wellness business after breast cancer and help others do the same.

Whether you're brand new or seasoned and ready to systemize, this book will meet you where you are. If you've ever said, "I don't know how to talk about this without sounding weird," or "I just wish someone would tell me what to post," then this is that guide.

And one more thing: I know you care about people. That's why you're here. You want to help. You want to make a difference. So let's make sure your message is reaching the people it's meant to serve.

Let's build a brand that doesn't just convert, but one that can duplicate. Because storytelling shouldn't just stop with you! It should spark something bigger.

~ Sydney Brown

1 - Your "Why I Joined" Story

Why This Story Matters:

This is the story that sets the emotional tone for everything else. It's not about impressing people. It's about relating to them. Done right, it makes your audience think, "That sounds like me."

People don't join perfect. They join real. And your "why I joined" story is how they figure out if you're the kind of person they could follow.

What This Story Does:

- Builds trust fast
- Frames you as relatable, not salesy
- Sets up your audience to care about what happens next
- Helps attract your kind of people (and gently repel the wrong fit)

Framework to Tell It:

1. **Before** – What was lifelike right before you found the opportunity?
   - Emotion: stuck, frustrated, hopeful, tired, lost, burned out, bored
2. **The Nudge** – What moment made you *look twice*?

   o   A comment, a social post, a product result, or
       someone you trusted
3. **The Hesitation** – What held you back (and what got
   you over it)?
   o   Doubts, fear of MLMs, time, money, burnout,
       pride, past failures
4. **The Leap** – What finally made you say yes?
   o   A vision, a gut feeling, an income goal, a
       bigger reason
5. **The Now** – What's changed since you started?
   o   Even if it's small (more hope, better sleep,
       new friends, purpose)

Real-Life Example:

"I wasn't looking for anything new. I was
working full-time, exhausted, and quietly
dreading Mondays. But when I saw my friend
post about how she finally had energy again
and was working from home, I couldn't stop
thinking about it. I rolled my eyes, of course. I'd
been burned before. But something about how
normal she was made me wonder…could this
work for me too? I stalked her for two weeks,
then finally messaged her at midnight. That was
9 months ago. I haven't replaced my income
yet, but I *have* replaced my hope. And
honestly? That matters more."

Swipeable Story Starters:

- "I was doing everything 'right' and still felt completely stuck."
- "I didn't join for the money. I joined because I couldn't stop thinking about it."
- "I said no at first. In fact, I said HELL no."
- "This wasn't part of the plan. But neither was feeling miserable every day."
- "I joined because I saw someone like me doing something different and I wanted in."

Tips:

- Keep it under 2 minutes spoken, three paragraphs written
- Choose *one* strong emotion to anchor your story
- Be specific. "I was exhausted from night shifts and Taco Bell runs" hits harder than "I was tired."
- Your honesty is your edge

$ Money Maker:

Mastering your "Why I Joined" story is pure gold because this is usually the first story people hear from you. If you're showing up on social media, going live, or answering "So what do you do?" in the DMs, this story sets the hook. If it's relatable, grounded, and told with just the right mix of honesty and hope, it makes people lean in.

They'll think:

- "That sounds like me."
- "They get it."
- "Maybe this could work for me, too."

And when people start thinking *that*, they start asking questions. They comment. They click your link. They message you. That's where the conversation begins. And conversations are what lead to conversions.

You don't need perfect graphics or a fancy funnel. You need a story that makes someone feel seen. This is it.

2 - The First Win Story

Why This Story Matters:

Your "first win" is the moment things clicked. The proof it wasn't just hype. It doesn't have to be huge. In fact, the smaller and more specific it is, the more relatable it becomes. This story builds belief. In you. In the product. In the process.

When someone hears your first win story, they stop wondering *if* it works and start thinking, '*what if* it worked for me, too?'

What This Story Does:

- Shifts your audience from skeptic to curious
- Demonstrates results without sounding braggy
- Creates momentum and relatability
- Gives social proof through storytelling

Framework to Tell It:

1. **The Setup** – What were you hoping for?
   - Better sleep, more energy, extra cash, a simple win
2. **The Test** – What did you try?
   - A product, a post, a conversation, an action step
3. **The Surprise** – What actually happened?

       ○ The outcome that made you pause and say, "Whoa, that worked."

4. **The Feeling** – How did it make you feel?
   ○ Seen, hopeful, validated, motivated
5. **The Share** – Why are you telling it now?
   ○ Because someone else is where you were, and they need to know it's real

Real-Life Example:

"I didn't join expecting magic. Honestly, I just wanted something to help with my sleep. I tried the blend my mentor suggested... figured it couldn't hurt. First night? Nothing. Second night? I slept straight through for the first time in months. I woke up feeling like I had a functioning brain again. That was the moment I realized this wasn't just oils and hype. This was hope in a bottle."

Swipeable Story Starters:

- "I wasn't sure it would do anything. But..."
- "The first time I knew this was real was when..."
- "I thought it was just a little thing. Until it wasn't."
- "It didn't take long. Just one message/post/product."
- "What surprised me most was how fast it happened."

Tips:

- Zoom in on one moment or one result
- Let the reader/viewer *feel* your surprise
- Avoid exaggerating... The truth is more powerful
- Don't wait for a six-figure win. The tiny ones matter more

$ Money Maker:

The first win story is the proof people need to lean in. Whether it's a product testimonial or a business moment, it builds **belief**, and *belief is what drives decisions.*

This story makes people think:

- "That's all it took?"
- "Wait... that's it? I could do that."
- "Huh. Maybe I should try it too."

It lowers the barrier. It kills the intimidation. It gives permission to start small and still expect something good. And when your audience starts thinking that way, they don't scroll past. They *click*. Or ask. Or order. And that, my friend, is where momentum begins.

3 - The Skeptic-to-Believer Story

Why This Story Matters:

Let's be real. Most people are skeptics when they hear about a product or opportunity. So were you, and that's why this story is powerful. It meets your audience exactly where they are. You're not preaching from a pedestal. You're reaching from experience.

This story gives people *permission* to be doubtful, but *inspiration* to be open. It's the perfect blend of "I get it" and "I changed my mind… here's why."

What This Story Does:

- Neutralizes objections without being pushy
- Builds empathy and trust
- Normalizes hesitation (which lowers pressure)
- Creates "if they changed their mind, maybe I can too" moments

Framework to Tell It:

1. **The Doubt** – What made you say "absolutely not" at first?
   - Bad experiences, MLM baggage, fear of being judged, pride
2. **The Pause** – What cracked the door open?

- A result you couldn't ignore, a friend's transformation, your curiosity

3. **The Turning Point** – What made you reconsider?
   - A personal win, a real convo, learning the facts, watching quietly for a while
4. **The Decision** – What helped you shift from "nah" to "maybe" to "I'm in"?
   - Trust, timing, validation, or finally hitting a personal breaking point
5. **The Belief** – What do you now know or feel that you didn't before?
   - That it works, that it's legit, that you're capable, that your pride was in the way

Real-Life Example:

"I said no for three years. THREE. I told my friend she was wasting her time, and I truly believed that. Until one day she paid cash for her vacation. I watched her kids grow up with her at home. I saw her glow up from the inside out. And one night, after my third glass of wine and a particularly crappy day at work, I messaged her: 'Okay. I'm listening.' That was the beginning of everything changing."

Swipeable Story Starters:

- "I swore I'd never join something like this."

- "I used to roll my eyes when people posted about this."
- "I had every excuse in the book… until I ran out."
- "It took me way longer than I like to admit."
- "If you told me a year ago I'd be doing this, I would've laughed."

Tips:

- Don't rush the transformation. Let the doubt breathe.
- Focus on how *you* changed your mind, not how someone "convinced" you
- Be relatable, not defensive
- Show that skepticism is normal, not a character flaw

$ Money Maker:

This story is your secret weapon when you're talking to fence-sitters. It's not a rebuttal. It's a mirror.

People don't like being told they're wrong. But they love hearing about someone who felt the exact same way… and came out the other side better for it.

This story lowers defenses. It builds safety. It makes people say, "That's literally me." And once they feel seen, not judged, they're more open to learning, asking, and trying.

Your skeptic story doesn't make you weak. It makes you trustworthy. And trust is the bridge to every order, every sign-up, every yes.

4 - The Product That Changed Everything

Why This Story Matters:

In a world of endless options and side-eye skepticism, people want proof...not perfection. This story is the testimonial that sticks. It's personal, vivid, and rooted in your own transformation (big or small). When people hear how one product shifted your life, even just a little, they start to believe it could do the same for them.

This isn't about ingredients and clinical studies. This is about the moment something finally *worked*, and made you *feel* like maybe everything could change.

What This Story Does:

- Makes your product real and emotional
- Moves people from curious to committed
- Sparks "tell me more" conversations
- Becomes the bridge to consistent referrals and repeat orders

Framework to Tell It:

1. **The Struggle** – What were you dealing with before?
   ○ Exhaustion, breakouts, overwhelm, sleep issues, stress, etc.
2. **The Try** – How did you use the product?

o What did you take, apply, or do?

3. **The Moment** – What shifted, and how did you know?
   o What result caught your attention and made it personal?
4. **The Ripple** – What happened after that?
   o Did your routine change? Did you tell someone? Order again?
5. **The Now** – How is life different because of that one product?
   o Confidence, comfort, joy, energy, peace of mind, ripple effects

Real-Life Example:

"I had tried everything for my brain fog. Coffee, pills, naps, journaling... nothing really stuck. I finally tried a blend my teammate swore by. I expected nothing. But on day three, I remembered my grocery list without writing it down. I didn't cry in traffic. I started sleeping better. It felt like I got pieces of myself back. That's the moment I knew this wasn't just a product. It was my way out of survival mode."

Swipeable Story Starters:

- "I honestly didn't expect this to work, but it did."
- "It started with one little product I wasn't even sure I believed in."

- "I tried it half-heartedly… and then everything shifted."
- "That one thing? Game changer."
- "I wasn't looking for magic. But it felt a little like it."

Tips:

- Keep the spotlight on *one* product
- Describe the *before* clearly so the after feels real
- Include the sensory: taste, smell, relief, and emotion
- Keep the tone "this worked for me," not "this will fix you."

$ Money Maker:

Your product story is a sales tool in disguise. It's not a pitch. It's a personal reveal. That one moment of honesty can drive more curiosity, shares, and reorders than a hundred fact sheets ever could.

When someone hears your product story and sees themselves in it, they don't need convincing. They need a cart link.

This is the story people screenshot. The one they send to a friend. The one they comment "Omg I need this" under.

Get good at telling it, and the product won't just change your life. It'll change your income too.

5 - The "Stuck" Story

Why This Story Matters:

Before someone joins your team or buys your product, they're often stuck. Stuck in a job, a mindset, a routine, or a cycle they don't love but can't seem to break. Sharing your "stuck" story shows them they're not alone. More importantly, that it's possible to get *unstuck* without having it all figured out first.

This story reminds people that it's okay to want more. And it shows them that starting messy is still starting.

What This Story Does:

- Builds deep emotional connection
- Shows people they're not broken or behind
- Positions your opportunity as a door, not a demand
- Makes your journey feel approachable, not intimidating

Framework to Tell It:

1. **The Cycle** – What did your "stuck" season look like?
   ○ Same routine, burnout, emotional spiral, financial pressure, playing small
2. **The Cracks** – What started to feel unbearable?
   ○ Anxiety, restlessness, missing out, Sunday dread, shame, numbness

3. **The Moment** – What made you whisper, "There has to be more than this"?
   - A meltdown, a message, a bill, a conversation, a random reel that hit too hard
4. **The Spark** – What tiny action did you take?
   - Clicking a link, asking a question, trying a sample, joining quietly
5. **The Shift** – What happened that reminded you you're not stuck forever?
   - A mindset flip, a goal met, a new connection, momentum

Real-Life Example:

"My life was... fine. That's the part that killed me. It was fine. I had a job, a routine, a relationship, and I felt guilty for wanting more. But I was quietly miserable. Every Sunday night felt like a countdown to death. One night, I saw a woman on Instagram talking about how she got her spark back by saying yes to something completely outside her comfort zone. I sat on it for a week. Then I asked for more info. That one message was my rebellion. And my rescue."

Swipeable Story Starters:

- "I was stuck in a life that looked okay on the outside."
- "I didn't even know how bad it had gotten... until I couldn't fake it anymore."
- "Every week felt like rinse and repeat... and I **hated** it."
- "I didn't want to settle. But I didn't know how to change, either."
- "This didn't start with motivation. It started with exhaustion."

Tips:

- Let people feel the emotion. Don't skip to the solution too fast
- Avoid trying to be the hero. Be the human
- Highlight the *first* step you took, not the 50th
- Speak to the person who's quietly spiraling, not loudly chasing

$ Money Maker:

This story speaks to the silent majority... the people scrolling in bed wondering if their life will ever feel better than "just okay." And guess what? That's your audience.

When you tell this story well, it's not just a confession. It's an invitation. It's what gets someone to comment, "this hit hard," or message you, "how did you know I needed this?"

You don't need to be perfect. You need to be honest.

This story gives your business meaning. And it gives your people permission to believe there's still more waiting for them, too.

6 - The "I Almost Quit" Story

Why This Story Matters:

This story brings vulnerability to the front of the room. It's the one that says, "I've doubted this too… and I'm still here." Whether it was the tech, the silence, the comparison trap, or just a plain bad day... everyone hits a wall. This story is your way of saying, "Me too. But I didn't stop."

It's powerful because it shows people how to stay, not just how to start.

What This Story Does:

- Makes you human and relatable
- Normalizes the emotional rollercoaster of growth
- Shows people what resilience looks like in real time
- Builds leadership without sounding preachy

Framework to Tell It:

1. **The Trigger** – What made you almost quit?
   - A no-show, a rejection, overwhelm, burnout, crickets online, a "mean girl" moment
2. **The Spiral** – What thoughts started to creep in?
   - "Maybe I'm not cut out for this." "No one cares." "This is dumb."
3. **The Pause** – What stopped you from pulling the plug?

  - A message, a win, a reminder of your why, a team member, your future self
4. **The Recovery** – What helped you get back in motion?
  - A simple task, encouragement, perspective, choosing faith over fear
5. **The Lesson** – What did that low moment teach you?
  - That hard doesn't mean wrong. That progress is never perfect. That your comeback is louder than your doubt.

Real-Life Example:

"I was three weeks in and ready to walk away. I felt like a fool. I was posting, messaging, following scripts... and nothing. Not even a nibble. Then someone on my team said, 'What if your first win is just one day away?' It wasn't even deep. But it hit me. I decided to show up one more time... and that live brought me my first customer. I almost missed her. I'm so glad I didn't quit the day before the magic happened."

Swipeable Story Starters:

- "I was *this close* to walking away."
- "No one talks about the part where you cry in your car."
- "I thought about quitting. More than once."

- "I had a moment where I questioned *everything*."
- "The only reason I didn't quit is because…"

Tips:

- Keep it raw but encouraging
- Focus on *one* low moment, not all of them
- Show your bounce-back, even if it was messy
- Speak directly to the person currently thinking about quitting

$ Money Maker:

This story is what keeps your team together. It's what recruits remember when they hit their first wall. It's the story that breathes belief into someone hanging on by a thread.

You don't need to act like you've always had it figured out. You need to be someone who *got back up.*

This story builds a culture of staying. And when people stay? They grow. They refer. They rise. And that's when your business moves from quick wins to lasting legacy.

7 - The Team/Friendship Story

Why This Story Matters:

People think they're buying products or joining a business. But what they're *really* craving is connection. This story lets them feel what it's like to belong before they ever sign up.

You're not just sharing a friendship—you're offering a glimpse into the culture, the support, and the unexpected gift of being surrounded by people who *get it*.

This story shows your community is a place where people grow together, not just hustle alone.

What This Story Does:

- Creates emotional safety and belonging
- Helps people imagine themselves in your world
- Builds value beyond money or products
- Shows your business as fun, fulfilling, and people-first

Framework to Tell It:

1. **The Lone Wolf** – What did your social circle or support system look like before?
   - Isolated? Exhausted mom? Stuck in corporate? Quietly longing for sisterhood?

2. **The First Connection** – Who reached out or made you feel seen?
    o A teammate, upline, sideline, community call
3. **The Shift** – When did it feel like more than business?
    o Inside jokes, shared struggles, check-ins that weren't about sales
4. **The Win** – What moment made you stop and think, "These are my people"?
    o A group chat, a team gift, a random voice note that turned your day around
5. **The Vibe Now** – How has having this team changed your energy?
    o Confidence, friendship, fun, support, laughter, "I'm not alone anymore"

Real-Life Example:

"I didn't join this for friends. In fact, I told myself I didn't need more women in my life. But this team? They changed me. One of them checked in on me the day I had a panic attack. Another sent a card when my cat died. We've never met in person, but they feel like home. This isn't just about selling. This is about soul care, that I didn't even know I needed."

Swipeable Story Starters:

- "I didn't think I needed more friends... until I found these people."
- "This team is the part I never saw coming."
- "We talk business, but we talk life even more."
- "It's not the sales that made me stay. It's the people."
- "They've seen me at my best and my messiest... and they still show up."

Tips:

- Be real about the *unexpected* magic of community
- Focus on a small gesture or moment that felt huge
- Use words like "we," "us," and "together" to create shared energy
- Let people see themselves in your team before they join it

$ Money Maker:

People stay for the people.

Yes, products and comp plans matter. But *culture* is what creates stickiness. When someone hears your friendship story, they realize this business isn't just about selling something. It's about becoming someone, and doing it with a crew that actually cares.

This story is your retention tool. It's your secret weapon for attracting the ones who don't just want income… they want impact, joy, and connection too.

8 - The "It Wasn't Easy" Truth Bomb

Why This Story Matters:

Everyone loves a success story... but it's the truth-tellers who build trust. When you talk openly about what was hard, what was messy, or what didn't go as planned, people lean in. They don't want another polished pitch. They want permission to be imperfect while they grow.

This is the story that gives them that.

What This Story Does:

- Builds trust through transparency
- Normalizes setbacks and slow starts
- Shows the reality behind the results
- Inspires people to keep going, even when it's not smooth

Framework to Tell It:

1. **The Expectation** – What did you think it would be like?
   - Fast money, instant results, easy success
2. **The Reality Check** – What actually happened?
   - Crickets, confusion, tech issues, mindset battles, bad days
3. **The Reaction** – How did that make you feel?

- Frustrated, embarrassed, defeated, scared, like giving up
4. **The Shift** – What made you keep going?
   - A breakthrough, a reminder, a conversation, a new perspective
5. **The Growth** – How are you stronger because of it?
   - Grit, empathy, resilience, better skills, deeper mission

Real-Life Example:

"I came in thinking I'd hit the ground running. I had the background, the work ethic, the drive. But none of that prepared me for what this business would ask of me. I was crushed the first time someone ghosted me. I cried when my live flopped. But those moments made me better. They made me real. And they made me *ready.* I'm proud of what I've built... not because it was easy, but because I earned every bit of it."

Swipeable Story Starters:

- "Can I be honest? It wasn't easy."
- "They said it was simple. They didn't say it was *easy.*"
- "I've failed more times than I've succeeded... and I'm still here."
- "This is the part no one posts about."

- "What they don't show in the highlight reel is…"

Tips:

- Let people see the messy middle, not just the victory lap
- Speak to those silently struggling, not the ones already soaring
- Keep it real, not dramatic
- Celebrate the *strength* you gained, not just the outcome

$ Money Maker:

This story proves you're not just lucky... you're *lasting.*

Anyone can be excited on day one. But showing up after hard days? That's where credibility is built.

When you share your honest hurdles, you give your audience a soft place to land. They realize you're not perfect and that they don't have to be either.

This story makes people respect your journey, trust your voice, and believe they can succeed too… even if their path gets bumpy.

9 - The "Why I Chose This Company" Story

Why This Story Matters:

Your audience wants to know *why this one*. With so many opportunities out there, what made you say yes to this particular company? This story helps others feel confident and informed... like they're choosing something solid, not just getting pitched.

It also sets you apart without slamming anyone else. This is about alignment, not comparison.

What This Story Does:

- Builds trust with people considering the company
- Reinforces that your decision was thoughtful and values-based
- Positions you as a guide, not just a seller
- Gives your team a shared narrative to rally around

Framework to Tell It:

1. **The Search** – Were you looking for something new?
   - Burned out, curious, comparing options, feeling unaligned
2. **The Standouts** – What stood out about this company?

- Culture, ingredients, pay plan, people, transparency
3. **The Alignment** – What matched your values?
    - Simplicity, family-first, clean products, impact-driven
4. **The Moment** – What made you *know* this was the one?
    - A product experience, a message from a leader, reading the mission
5. **The Belief** – Why are you still here?
    - Results, community, fulfillment, personal growth

Real-Life Example:

"I'd seen a dozen opportunities in my feed. I was skeptical, honestly. But this one felt different. The ingredients were clean. The vibe was chill. The leadership was transparent. And the mission? That's what got me. I didn't feel like I was joining a company. I felt like I was joining a movement. I said yes with curiosity. I've stayed because it's changed everything."

Swipeable Story Starters:

- "I wasn't looking for a *company*... I was looking for *alignment*."
- "Here's why I chose *this one* out of everything out there."
- "I did my research. I asked questions. And then I said yes."

- "It wasn't the hype that convinced me. It was the heart."
- "The values matched mine. That's what mattered most."

Tips:

- Be specific about what drew you in
- Avoid tearing down other companies. Focus on what felt right for *you*
- Let your audience hear the decision-making process, not just the outcome
- Share your confidence, not pressure

$ Money Maker:

This story is your built-in credibility boost. It quiets the skepticism and answers the question, "Why this?" without them needing to ask.

When you tell it with clarity and heart, it becomes the permission slip others need to make a move.

This isn't just a good fit for you... it might be the *perfect* fit for them, too. And this story helps them see that.

10 - The Legacy Vision Story

Why This Story Matters:

Most people think they're signing up for some free samples or a side hustle. But what if they're actually saying yes to a life they never imagined possible?

This story is about zooming out. It's about painting the big picture. It's the difference between "I sell wellness" and "I'm creating a new future for my family."

It invites people to imagine something bigger for themselves, and that is where transformation begins.

What This Story Does:

- Connects your work to your *why*
- Inspires others to dream bigger, not just buy something
- Positions your brand as a movement, not just a moment
- Helps people emotionally invest in your long-term vision

Framework to Tell It:

1. **The Before** – What was life like before you said yes?
   - Financially, emotionally, lifestyle-wise

2. **The Shift** – What started to open your eyes to a different possibility?
   - ○ A pain point, a dream reignited, a story you heard
3. **The Vision** – What are you building now?
   - ○ Time freedom, legacy income, creative freedom, mobility, giving back
4. **The Ripple** – Who will benefit because you said yes?
   - ○ Your family, your kids, your team, your future self
5. **The Invitation** – What could *their* life look like too?
   - ○ End with a question or a gentle invitation to imagine more

Real-Life Example:

"I used to think I was destined to work until I died. I didn't grow up with options. I grew up with survival. But this? This gave me a crack in the door. I said yes to a discount and ended up saying yes to a legacy. I'm building something my son can be proud of. I'm chasing sunsets in places I've never been. And I'm helping other women remember they still get to dream. That's what this really is for me."

Swipeable Story Starters:

- "I said yes for the products... but stayed for the purpose."
- "This is about more than today. It's about what I'm building for tomorrow."
- "I wanted options. Now I'm building them."
- "The real win isn't what I've earned. It's what I've envisioned."
- "What if this was the bridge to your freedom, too?"

Tips:

- Make it personal, not perfect
- Speak to possibility, not pressure
- Keep your tone inspiring and open-hearted
- Let your audience feel like they're part of the vision

$ Money Maker:

Legacy stories activate long-term thinkers. These are the buyers who become lifers, the followers who become leaders.

When someone hears your big-picture vision, they start to imagine their own. That's how you turn curiosity into commitment.

This story helps you magnetize the ones who want to build, not just buy. And that is where the real income lives.

Top 10 Stories Workbook

Story 1: Your "Why I Joined" Story

Step 1: **What was life like right before you found this opportunity?**
(Think: tired, stuck, broke, overworked, skeptical, etc.)

✍️ **My BEFORE:**

Step 2: What gave you the NUDGE to look twice?

Was it a person, a post, a product, a result? Be specific.

✍️ **My NUDGE:**

Step 3: What made you hesitate... and what helped you get past that?

Fear, pride, bad past experience? Then what shifted?

✍️ **My HESITATION + BREAKTHROUGH:**

Step 4: What made you finally say YES?

A dream, a gut feeling, a deal, a moment?

✍️ **My REASON I SAID YES:**

Step 5: What's changed since then? (Even just a little!)

New friendships, better sleep, more hope, small wins…

✍🏻 **My NOW:**

Bonus Prompt:

In one sentence… what would you say to "past you" the day before you joined?

✍🏻 **Dear Past Me…**

Swipe + Remix:

Pick a starter and write your full story below:

- "I was doing everything 'right' and still felt completely stuck."
- "This wasn't part of the plan. But neither was feeling miserable every day."
- "I joined because I saw someone like me doing something different… and I wanted in."

✍️ **My Story (Draft):**

Story 2: The First Win Story

Step 1: What were you hoping for?

Better sleep? A little energy boost? A product win? A good convo? More confidence?

✍ My SETUP:

Step 2: What did you try?

Name the action. What was the moment you dipped your toe in?

✍ My TEST:

Step 3: What actually happened that surprised you?

Big or small, what happened that made you pause and go "...wait, that worked?"

✎☐ **My SURPRISE RESULT:**

Step 4: How did it make you feel?

Be honest. What shifted in your energy, your thinking, your belief?

✎☐ **My FEELING:**

Step 5: Why are you sharing this?

What would you tell someone who is still on the fence?

✍️ **My REASON FOR SHARING:**

Bonus Prompt:

In one sentence, how did this first win change your belief in the process?

✍️ **Before, I wasn't sure. But now…**

Swipe + Remix:

Choose a story starter and finish it in your own voice:

- "I wasn't sure it would do anything. But…"
- "It didn't take long. Just one message/post/product."
- "The first time I knew this was real was when…"

✍ ☐ **My Story (Draft):**

Story 3: The Skeptic-to-Believer Story

Step 1: What made you say "nope" at first?

Think of your earliest doubts or assumptions. Were you burned before? Judgy? Protective of your image?

✍🏻 **My DOUBT:**

Step 2: What cracked the door open?

What did you see, feel, or learn that made you curious?

✍🏻 **My PAUSE MOMENT:**

Step 3: What was the turning point that made you reconsider?

A real conversation, something you watched, a result you couldn't ignore… what softened you?

✍️ **My SHIFT:**

Step 4: What finally made you say "I'm in"?

What did it take to go from resistant to ready?

✍️ **My DECISION:**

Step 5: What do you believe now that you didn't before?

What have you proven to yourself?

✍☐ **My NEW BELIEF:**

Bonus Prompt:

What would you tell someone who feels the same way you once did?

✍☐ **If you're where I was, here's what I want you to know…**

Swipe + Remix:

Pick a starter and make it yours:

- "I swore I'd never join something like this."
- "I had every excuse in the book... until I ran out."
- "If you told me a year ago I'd be doing this, I would've laughed."

✍ **My Story (Draft):**

Story 4: The Product That Changed Everything

Step 1: What were you struggling with before?

Be specific. Brain fog, blemishes, stress, low energy, overwhelm, pain, etc. Be sure to use terms that are not considered medical diagnoses, but rather symptoms. (For example: say blemishes or breakouts instead of acne.)

✍️ My STRUGGLE:

Step 2: What product did you try, and how?

Name the product and how you used it. Daily? Topically? In a smoothie? Under your tongue?

✍️ My TRY:

Step 3: What shifted that made you stop and notice?

Describe the moment that made you go, "Whoa... this is working."

✍☐ **My MOMENT:**

Step 4: What ripple effect did that change create?

What happened next? More energy? A new habit? People asking questions?

✍☐ **My RIPPLE EFFECT:**

Step 5: How is your life different now, even in a small way?

How did this one thing help you feel more like you again?

✍️ **My NOW:**

Bonus Prompt:

If you could only tell one person about this product, what would you say?

✍️ **My QUICK PITCH (without sounding salesy):**

Swipe + Remix:

Choose a line to jumpstart your story:

- "I honestly didn't expect this to work, but it did."
- "It started with one little product I wasn't even sure I believed in."
- "That one thing? Game changer."

✍️ My Story (Draft):

Story 5: The "Stuck" Story

Step 1: What did your stuck season look like?

Describe the cycle you felt trapped in. Routines?
Exhaustion? Lack of purpose?

✍ My CYCLE:

Step 2: What started to feel unbearable?

What were the cracks in the surface? Be honest.
What kept you up at night or drained you the most?

✍ My CRACKS:

Step 3: What was the moment that made you whisper, "There has to be more than this"?

Was it a specific event, feeling, or trigger?

✍☐ My MOMENT:

Step 4: What tiny action did you take?

What was the first little move? A click? A message? A decision?

✍☐ My SPARK:

Step 5: What happened that reminded you you're not stuck forever?

How did things begin to shift, even just a little?

✍︎ **My SHIFT:**

Bonus Prompt:

What would you say to someone stuck in the same cycle you were in?

✍︎ **Dear You, I Know What That Feels Like…**

Swipe + Remix:

Choose a story starter and finish it your way:

- "I was stuck in a life that looked okay on the outside."
- "Every week felt like rinse and repeat... and I *hated* it."
- "I didn't want to settle. But I didn't know how to change, either."

✍️ **My Story (Draft):**

Story 6: The "I Almost Quit" Story

Step 1: What made you almost walk away?

Describe the moment, trigger, or experience that made you want to quit.

✍️ My TRIGGER:

Step 2: What were the thoughts running through your head?

Be honest. What did your inner critic say?

✍️ My SPIRAL:

Step 3: What stopped you from giving up completely?

What or who reminded you to pause instead of pulling the plug?

✍️ My PAUSE MOMENT:

Step 4: What did you do to get yourself back in motion?

Even the smallest action counts here. What helped you bounce back?

✍️ My RECOVERY:

Step 5: What did that experience teach you?

What insight, strength, or shift came from that almost-quit moment?

✍️ **My LESSON:**

Bonus Prompt:

What would you say to someone who's having their "I almost quit" moment right now?

✍️ **Hey, I Know That Feeling…**

Swipe + Remix:

Use one of these lines to kick off your story:

- "I was *this close* to walking away."
- "No one talks about the part where you cry in your car."
- "The only reason I didn't quit is because…"

✍☐ My Story (Draft):

Story 7: The Team/Friendship Story

Step 1: What did your circle look like before?

Describe how connected (or not) you felt before
joining your team.

✍☐ My BEFORE:

Step 2: Who made you feel seen early on?

Was it a message, a comment, a warm welcome?

✍☐ My FIRST CONNECTION:

Step 3: When did it start feeling like *more* than business?

What moment gave you that "these are my people" feeling?

🔥 **My SHIFT:**

Step 4: What moment or memory made you feel like part of something?

Share the group chat, laugh, gift, or conversation that stood out.

🔥 **My TEAM WIN:**

Step 5: How has this community changed your energy?

Think: confidence, joy, accountability, purpose, or feeling seen.

✍️ **My NOW VIBE:**

Bonus Prompt:

What would you say to someone craving connection like you were?

✍️ **Hey, I Didn't Know I Needed This Either...**

Swipe + Remix:

Choose a starter to help shape your story:

- "I didn't think I needed more friends... until I met them."
- "This team is the thing I didn't even know I was missing."
- "We talk life more than sales—and that's what I love."

✍️ My Story (Draft):

Story 8: The "It Wasn't Easy" Truth Bomb

Step 1: What were you expecting?

Share what you thought this would be like. Fast growth? Easy path?

✍️ **My EXPECTATION:**

Step 2: What was the real experience?

Be honest. What actually happened early on?

✍️ **My REALITY CHECK:**

Step 3: How did that make you feel?

What emotions came up? What did you start to believe?

✍ My REACTION:

Step 4: What kept you from quitting?

What helped you push through that hard season?

✍ My SHIFT:

Step 5: How did this experience make you stronger?

What traits or mindset shifts did you gain?

✍️ **My GROWTH:**

Bonus Prompt:

If someone feels like it's too hard, what do you want them to know?

✍️ **It's Okay If You're In That Place Too...**

Swipe + Remix:

Choose one to jumpstart your story:

- "They said it would be simple… but they didn't say it would be easy."
- "No one talks about the messy middle, so here's mine."
- "I've had more flops than wins some weeks—and I'm still here."

✍️ **My Story (Draft):**

Story 9: The "Why I Chose This Company" Story

Step 1: What were you looking for before this?

Were you burnt out, curious, or searching for something more aligned?

✍️ My SEARCH:

Step 2: What stood out right away?

Think: products, people, pay plan, transparency, vibe.

✍️ My STANDOUTS:

Step 3: What matched your values?

What made this feel like it just *fit*?

✍☐ **My ALIGNMENT:**

Step 4: What moment sealed the deal?

Describe the turning point where you *knew* this was the one.

✍☐ **My DECISION MOMENT:**

Step 5: Why are you still here?

Results, community, purpose, personal growth?

✍☐ **My BELIEF:**

Bonus Prompt:

What do you want someone curious about this company to know?

✍☐ **If You're Wondering If This Is a Fit…**

Swipe + Remix:

Pick one to spark your storytelling:

- "Here's why I chose this company... and why I've stayed."
- "It wasn't just the products. It was the mission."
- "I never thought I'd join something like this... until it felt like home."

✍️ My Story (Draft):

Story 10: The Legacy Vision Story

Step 1: What was your life like before?

Financially, emotionally, or day-to-day lifestyle...
paint the picture.

🔊 My BEFORE:

Step 2: What made you start to dream differently?

Was it burnout, a desire for more, or something
someone said?

🔊 My SHIFT:

Step 3: What vision are you building now?

Time freedom? Travel? Options for your family?
Creative independence?

✍ ☐ **My VISION:**

Step 4: Who benefits from this choice you made?

Think about the ripple effect: your kids, team,
community, future self.

✍ ☐ **My RIPPLE:**

Step 5: What do you want others to imagine for themselves?

Use your story to help them picture something new for *their* life.

🔓 **My INVITATION:**

Bonus Prompt:

What future are you excited about that you never thought possible before?

🔓 **My NEW FUTURE LOOKS LIKE…**

Swipe + Remix:

Use one of these to launch your Legacy Story:

- "I didn't know I was building a legacy. I just thought I was trying something new."
- "This business gave me the courage to imagine a future I'd never let myself want."
- "I'm not just chasing success. I'm creating options."

✍☐ My Story (Draft):

Story Strategy Cheat Sheet (by story)

✦ 1. Your Origin Story

When to use: Right when someone meets you or asks how you got started. Great for social posts, bios, or first convos.
Why it works: It builds an instant connection and shows you're not some overnight success. They'll trust your journey more.

✦ 2. The Skeptic-to-Believer Story

When to use: Anytime someone's on the fence. DM convos, lives, FAQs, or in your caption.
Why it works: It validates their hesitation but shows the transformation is real.

✦ 3. The Product That Changed Everything

When to use: Whenever you're recommending a product or answering "what's your favorite?"
Why it works: It turns a product pitch into a personal moment.

✦ 4. The First Win Story

When to use: When someone's feeling like they haven't had a big success yet, or when you're showing that the little wins *matter*.
Why it works: It proves that momentum starts small. That first order, first "yes," or first commission is a powerful motivator, and your audience needs to know it counts.

✦ 5. The "Stuck" Story

When to use: When you sense someone is frozen in fear, self-doubt, or overthinking.

Why it works: It helps them feel seen and supported, not pushed.

✦ 6. The "I Almost Quit" Story

When to use: When someone says they're discouraged, or during a live where you want to keep it real.
Why it works: It's vulnerable, and vulnerability is magnetic.

✦ 7. The Team/Friendship Story

When to use: When someone says they're craving community, or you're sharing about your tribe online.
Why it works: We're all wired for belonging. This taps that.

✦ 8. The "It Wasn't Easy" Truth Bomb

When to use: After you've hit a milestone or rank, be the one who tells the truth behind the win.
Why it works: It builds trust, not envy.

✦ 9. The "Why I Chose This Company" Story

When to use: During a recruiting convo or in a curiosity post.
Why it works: It answers the big "why this one?" without sounding salesy.

✦ 10. The Legacy Vision Story

When to use: In deeper convos, long-form posts, or vision-casting calls.
Why it works: It invites people to dream bigger alongside you.

✦ 11. Their Story *(yes! This one's **not** about you!)*
When to use: Ask them questions that help *them* step into a story of possibility.

Why it works: People don't join your dream. They join because it reflects theirs.

You don't have to "close" people. You just have to connect.

You don't have to be fancy. You just have to be *you.*

These stories are tools in your belt, not rules on a script. Use what fits, skip what doesn't, remix and repeat. The goal? Make people feel something. Then invite them into more.

And now? Go tell it.

The Network Marketer's Real-World Toolkit

So you've got your stories down, you're vibing with your voice, and you're ready to connect. But now what?

Let's toss in the real-deal magic: what to actually *do* with these stories and how to turn connections into conversions without becoming *That Pushy Person.*

When to Use Each Story (by phase)

You've got ten stories. But how do they fit into your real conversations? Here's a guide to plug them into your process:

Prospecting & Inviting

- **The Origin Story:** Share how you got started and what drew you in. Perfect for intros and bios.
- **The Skeptic-to-Believer Story:** For fence-sitters and the quietly curious.
- **The "Stuck" Story:** Helps people who feel frozen see a way forward.

Presenting

- **The Product That Changed Everything: Personalize** your product pitch with heart.
- **The First Win Story:** Share those early, small wins to build belief.

Overcoming Objections

- **The "I Almost Quit" Story:** Shows resilience and makes the process real.
- **The "It Wasn't Easy" Truth Bomb:** Pull back the curtain on what success really took.

Closing & Follow-Up

- **The Team/Friendship Story:** Offer a glimpse into the community behind the business.
- **The "Why I Chose This Company" Story:** Gives clarity on alignment without pressure.

Long-Term Engagement

- **The Legacy Vision Story:** Paint the big picture of what you're building and invite others to imagine theirs.

These aren't scripts. They're connection points. And when used at the right moment, they feel natural, authentic, and even fun.

Make a note card. Highlight your favorites. Practice aloud. Soon, this will feel like second nature.

Top 10 Objections + Personality-Aligned Responses

Let's be real. Objections happen. And when you know someone's color personality, you can respond in a way that actually lands. Here's how to handle the 10 most common objections across all four types:

1. "I'm not a salesperson."

- **Yellow (Helper/Heart):** "Perfect. This isn't about pushing people. It's about helping them find something that matters. That's what you already do naturally."
- **Red (Boss / Bottom-Line):** "Perfect. You're not here to chit-chat. You're here to win. People follow strong voices, not scripts."
- **Green (Engineer/Thinker):** "Sales isn't the goal. Sharing useful information is. You're just helping someone solve a problem with logic and facts."
- **Blue (Social Butterfly):** "Ha! I'm always chatting, but I don't *sell* either. I just share cool stuff I love...and people ask."

2. "I don't have time."

- **Yellow:** "I get it. But helping just one person a week is still something. That's what fills my cup."
- **Red:** "You don't make excuses, you make moves. This builds leverage so your time works for you."

- **Green:** "I can show you the actual time commitment, broken down with real examples. It's more efficient than it looks."
- **Blue:** "Oh I hear you. I squeezed it in between convos. If you've got five minutes between chats, you've got enough to start."

3. "I don't have money."

- **Yellow:** "I felt that too. But when I realized this could help people *and* lighten my load, I made room for it."
- **Red:** "Then you definitely need this. This is about making your money hustle for you."
- **Green:** "Let's map out the numbers and look at the return. You're already spending money somewhere. This just reallocates it wisely."
- **Blue:** "Totally been there. I just grabbed the smallest thing, shared it, and it paid for itself fast."

4. "I need to think about it."

- **Yellow:** "Of course. You're thoughtful, and I respect that. I'll check in later if that's okay."
- **Red:** "Winners don't overthink. You know if it's a yes or no. Trust your gut and take the lead."
- **Green:** "Makes total sense. I've got some details and breakdowns I can send you. It'll help you make a smart call."
- **Blue:** "Honestly? You're usually fast to decide. If it's a no, cool. If it's a yes, I'll help you run with it."

5. "I've done something like this before and it didn't work."

- **Yellow:** "That happened to me too. But this time, I wasn't alone. The support made all the difference."

- **Red:** "I get that. But this is built different…and it's working."
- **Green:** "Let's compare what didn't work and see how this stacks up. I think you'll see the difference."
- **Blue:** "Honestly? Same. But something about this just clicked different for me."

6. "My partner wouldn't go for it."

- **Yellow:** "Mine was hesitant too, until they saw how happy it made me."
- **Red:** "If it's helping you win, they'll come around. Do they need extra information?"
- **Green:** "Here's what helped me walk mine through the logic. Want a copy?"
- **Blue:** "I told mine I was just going to test it. No pressure. Now they're on board."

7. "It feels like a pyramid scheme."

- **Yellow:** "I totally get why that sounds weird. I only joined because it felt safe and human."
- **Red:** "This isn't about recruiting tons of people. It's about results. Real product, real value."
- **Green:** "Let's define what a pyramid scheme is and how this legally isn't. I'll show you."
- **Blue:** "I thought that too. Until I saw the structure and realized how different it really is."

8. "I'm not a social media person."

- **Yellow:** "Some of the best stories happen offline. People want to connect, not scroll."
- **Red:** "You can still win. Use texts, calls, whatever works. The goal is results."

- **Green:** "There are private ways to do this. I've got examples of low-visibility approaches." *
- **Blue:** "Honestly? Me either. But I just tried one thing at a time."

9. "I'm not confident enough."

- **Yellow:** "You don't have to be loud. Just be real. People feel that."
- **Red:** "Confidence grows with action. Start small, build fast."
- **Green:** "Structure builds confidence. Let me show you how we support that."
- **Blue:** "I started by watching and listening. It gave me time to warm up."

10. "I'm just not sure if it's for me."

- **Yellow:** "That's okay. But I saw something in you, and wanted to offer it."
- **Red:** "You'll know when you're ready. Winners usually feel it before they believe it."
- **Green:** "Let's go through the checklist. If it doesn't match, no harm done."
- **Blue:** "I said the same thing. Then I saw one story and felt differently."

This isn't about overcoming objections. It's about meeting people where they are.

Speak their language. Tell your truth. The rest will all fall into place.

10 Low-Visibility Approaches

(for "I'm not a social media person" Greens)

1. **One-on-One Coffee Chats or Zooms**
   Quiet, focused conversations where questions are welcomed and no pressure exists.

2. **Detailed Follow-Up Emails**
   Thoughtfully written emails with links, product PDFs, ingredient lists, or FAQ sheets.

3. **Text Message Check-ins**
   Simple, respectful text conversations that allow for paced interaction.

4. **Referral Cards or Samples**
   Printed or digital cards you hand out or send in the mail. Great for low-tech interactions.

5. **Resource Library/Dropbox Folder**
   Create a private folder with data sheets, testimonials, and documents they can browse on their own time.

6. **Invite-Only Info Sessions**
   Small, quiet gatherings online or in-person where a few curious folks can ask questions.

7. **Voice Notes or Video Messages (1:1)**
   A personal message that feels high-touch but still

private and optional.

8. **Silent Shopping Links**

Share direct links to curated product bundles. No funnel, no fanfare, just click and learn.

9. **Lead with Product Use**

Casually use products in front of friends/family and offer info only if they ask. Let curiosity lead.

10. **Private Messenger Threads (Messenger/WhatsApp/Signal)**

Ongoing, calm conversations that allow for deeper dialogue without a newsfeed in sight.

The Smooth Close Framework

In MLM, we don't "sell" people. We walk them through a journey of understanding. Here's how to apply a classic 5-step close:

1. Get an Appointment

Use curiosity and short invites: "If I showed you something that could make your life easier and healthier, would you want to know about it?"

2. Build Rapport

Ask questions, listen, and make it about them. Use your stories to bridge the connection.

3. Give a One-Minute Presentation

Stick to a short message: who you are, what you found, what it's doing for others.

4. Ask a Closing Question

Simple and no-pressure: "Would this be something you'd want to try if it helped you feel better?"

5. Handle Objections (if any)

Use the responses we outline in the next section based on their personality.

Objection Handling... with Story

Tired of sounding like a script bot? Use these story flips instead:

Objection: "I'm not a salesperson."
Try this: "I said the same thing. I just shared what worked for me, and people leaned in. My first win? It came from being honest, not salesy."

Objection: "I don't have time."
Try this: "I didn't either. But I wanted more time *freedom*, and five minutes a day slowly added up. This isn't about time. It's about freedom and choices."

Objection: "I've tried things like this before."
Try this: "Same. I was burned out, skeptical, and done. But this felt different, and the support here changed everything."

Personality-Based Closing Case Studies

Red Personality (Boss / Bottom-Line)

Scenario: A high achiever who wants control and speed.

You say: "Look, I know you don't need fluff. If you want a system that puts you in the driver's seat and actually pays, I'll show you exactly how fast you can hit the ground running."

Blue Personality (Social Butterfly)

Scenario: A life-of-the-party type who talks a mile a minute.

You say: "You already talk to everyone! Imagine getting paid for being your outgoing, awesome self. This would fit your vibe perfectly…and it's fun."

Green Personality (Engineer / Thinker)

Scenario: A calm, detail-oriented person who needs all the facts.

You say: "I get it. You want the blueprint. Let me send over a breakdown and FAQs. We'll walk through your questions and build a plan that feels smart and steady."

Yellow Personality (Helper / Heart)

Scenario: A nurturing, service-oriented person who wants to feel good about what they do.

You say: "You'd be so good at this because people trust you. This isn't about selling. It's about helping others feel better. And you're already doing that."

The 4 Buyer Types + Your Go-To Story

1. The Researcher – GREEN Personality
Loves details and data. Give them:
- ✓ *Why I Chose This Company*
- ✓ *It Wasn't Easy Truth Bomb*

2. The Feeler – YELLOW Personality
Driven by emotion, connection, vibes. Give them:
- ✓ *Legacy Vision*
- ✓ *Team/Friendship Story*

3. The Social Butterfly – BLUE Personality
Thrives on connection, excitement, and shared enthusiasm. Give them:
- ✓ *Origin Story*
- ✓ *First Win Story*

4. The Action-Taker – RED Personality
Moves fast, needs a spark. Give them:
- ✓ *Skeptic-to-Believer Story*
- ✓ *Product That Changed Everything*

Quick DM Flow Using Stories

1. Start with a curiosity hook
2. Ask a micro-question (low-stakes, easy to answer)
3. Drop a 1–2 sentence story nugget
4. Ask if they'd like more info

   Example: "I used to crash every afternoon. Switched to [product] on a whim and now I'm back to feeling human. You ever tried anything like that before?"

Boom. Story. Question. Connection.

10 Ways to Use These Stories Online

1. **Carousel Graphics on Instagram or Facebook**
    Break a story into bite-sized slides for visual impact and easy engagement.

2. **TikTok or Reels with Voiceover**
    Tell your story in short, punchy formats. Use your voice or captions to narrate.

3. **Email Blasts or Newsletter Series**
    Share one story at a time in a weekly series that builds connection and keeps people opening.

4. **Facebook Live (or Instagram Live)**
    Walk through a story in real time as part of a product intro or business connection session.

5. **Team Welcome Docs or Onboarding Trainings**
    Use your core stories to model authenticity and build belief from day one.

6. **Testimonials That Don't Feel Cringe**
    Convert stories into natural, compelling social proof without sounding like an infomercial.

7. **Slides for a Zoom Presentation or Quick Pitch**
    Use your stories to create a 3-slide intro for any virtual chat or group presentation.

8. **Pinned Content on Your Profiles**
    Turn one strong story into a pinned post or

highlight that serves as a silent recruiter.

9. **Story Highlights or Guides on Instagram**
   Organize story types (product, mission, transformation) into themed IG highlights or guide collections.

10. **Voice Memos or Direct Messages**
    Send a short version of a story in a private chat or voice message. Great for 1:1 curiosity convos.

Story Mapping for Your New People

When someone joins your team, help them map their story.

Here's a simple guide. Escalate if their goals dictate faster education:

- Day 1: "Why I Said Yes"
- Week 2: "My First Win"
- Month 1: "How This Changed Me"
- Month 3: "Who I'm Becoming"

This helps them feel part of something. And they'll always have a story to tell.

30 Days of Prompts Using These Stories

For this, I'm actually going to recommend you get a journal or notebook and, at least for a little while, take up "journaling."

To craft a truly great story, you need to speak your truth. If you drop knee-jerk responses into a template, your prospects will be able to see through the lack of authenticity. I urge you to spend some time (5-15 minutes a day) reflecting on these prompts.

For now, this information is for no one but you. Once you get real with yourself, you can then decide what information would be beneficial for your prospect to know.

1. Your Origin Story (why I joined)

- **The Spark:** When exactly did the product/solution catch your attention?

- **Before & After:** What were you struggling with before making the switch?

- **The Turning Point:** Describe vividly the day or moment you committed fully.

2. First Win

- **First Taste of Success:** What was your first successful experience selling or sharing your product?

- **Validation Moment:** How did feedback from a customer prove this was the right path?

- **Confidence Booster:** What small achievement first convinced you this was doable?

3. Skeptic-to-Believer

- **Initial Doubt:** Describe your initial skepticism about the products or business model.

- **Proof Moment:** What exact experience convinced you to change your mind?

- **Mindset Shift:** How did overcoming your doubts strengthen your belief?

4. Product That Changed Everything

- **Discovery Moment:** When and how did you discover the game-changing product?

- **Immediate Impact:** What noticeable results did you experience right away?

- **Why It's Essential:** Why do you now recommend it above anything else?

5. Stuck Story

- **The Rut:** Describe a time when you felt stuck or frustrated in life.

- **Breaking Free:** How exactly did your product or opportunity help break that pattern?

- **Life After:** What's the tangible difference in your life after becoming unstuck?

6. I Almost Quit Story

- **Behind-the-Scenes Challenge:** What major obstacle nearly made you quit?

- **Real Talk Moment:** Share an honest, raw experience you don't normally reveal.

- **The Comeback:** How did you overcome a major setback?

7. Team/Friendship Story

- **The Bonding Moment:** Describe the moment you felt genuinely connected to your team.

- **Supportive Interaction:** Share a specific instance when your team helped you through something challenging.

- **Why Community Matters:** What does the team or friendship aspect add to your life beyond the business?

8. The "It Wasn't Easy" Truth Bomb

- **Your Reality Check:** What unexpected challenge or moment of doubt nearly stopped you in your tracks?
- **Resilience Moment:** How did you push through, pivot, or find clarity?
- **What It Proves:** Why is this moment something people need to hear—not just the polished wins?

9. Social Proof Story

- **Customer Buzz:** Share a favorite testimonial or enthusiastic review that surprised or moved you.

- **Group Excitement:** Recall a social moment or event where your product created noticeable excitement or positive chatter.

- **Influencer Endorsement:** Have you had a relatable or influential person genuinely praise your product? What did that feel like?

10. Legacy Vision

- **Your Deeper Why:** What's the ultimate impact you dream of making?

- **Personal Inspiration:** Who specifically inspires your vision, and why?

- **Future Snapshot:** How is your life different five years from now if you achieve your goal?

You've got the stories. You've got the system. You've got the heart.

This isn't about pitching. This is about planting seeds with your story and letting them grow.

Conclusion

Look, here's the deal: you've got the stories now, you've got the prompts, and you've got the map laid out clearly in front of you. But here's something crucial I want you to remember...this is so much bigger than just a handful of clever tales to sprinkle into your social media feed. This is about shaping the direction of your life and about stepping into a future that's built around passion, purpose, and true authenticity.

Let's be honest for a minute. No one wakes up one day magically inspired and totally fearless. We all start from somewhere messy, unsure, and probably at least a little uncomfortable. That's exactly where the best stories come from. They rise out of those real moments! Yes! The ones filled with self-doubt, messy hair days, and maybe even the occasional ugly cry. You've been there; I've been there. (Who am I kidding, sometimes I'm still there, navigating through life's curveballs.)

The difference is that now you know how to leverage these experiences to inspire others. Your journey has equipped you with the power to reach people exactly where they're at. Whether they're skeptics, social butterflies, researchers, or action-takers, you've got something valuable to offer. You've learned to speak their language, meet them in their stories, and pull them gently, yet confidently, toward something better.

Think about it: how many times have you scrolled through your phone, searching for a connection or some small spark of inspiration? How often have you wished someone would just be real, honest, and genuinely invested in helping you get unstuck? That's who you get to be for others now.

You're no longer just sharing products or business opportunities. You're shaping legacies, sparking friendships, and building genuine community. Your stories are seeds planted in fertile soil. Every single post, every conversation, every brave "truth bomb" you drop is nurturing growth in someone else's life. And, by extension, your own.

But here's the catch (because there's always a catch, right?): these stories only come to life if you tell them. They don't serve anyone sitting quietly in your drafts folder or hidden in your notebook. It's going to take courage to hit publish, to speak openly, and to risk vulnerability. And yes, it might feel uncomfortable at first, maybe even terrifying. But bravery is just fear with better marketing. Embrace the nerves. They mean you're doing something significant.

So, here's my ask for you: commit today! Yup; *right now*, to becoming an active storyteller. Lean into the imperfection, embrace the messy authenticity, and know deep in your bones that your words have real power. Trust me, someone out there desperately needs exactly what you've got to offer, delivered in precisely the way only you can deliver it.

Envision yourself a year from now, having stepped fully into your purpose, celebrating not just financial milestones or sales records (though those are fun too!), but real, heartfelt impacts; messages of gratitude from customers whose lives you've genuinely enhanced, teammates thanking you for believing in them when nobody else did, and your own quiet moments of reflection realizing just how far you've come.

That's the legacy you're building. That's the story worth telling.

So yes, use the prompts I've given you. Craft each story carefully and intentionally. But never lose sight of the heartbeat behind them. Every prompt is an invitation, every story a bridge, every interaction a potential lifeline. You are doing so much more than marketing; you're creating ripple effects of goodness, healing, and hope.

This is your moment to say "yes" to a future bigger and brighter than you've ever allowed yourself to dream. You deserve that. Your audience deserves that. The world deserves that. Show up boldly, consistently, and authentically... *and watch the magic unfold.*

Remember, you're not doing this alone. I'm cheering you on every step of the way. We've got big things ahead. Let's go tell some amazing stories and change some lives, starting today!

~ Syd

Ready to Get to Work?

Free Gift Membership!

Congratulations! You have a lot to be proud of and a lot of stories to tell. I'd like to invite you to join me and my storytelling friends as we learn, grow, practice without judgment, and continue on this great journey of life.

You are formally invited to join us in the *Just BS Community*. Oh, come on now! What did you think that stood for?

We're a growing community of Basic (or Badass, you decide) Storytellers.

Some stick to *telling* their stories, and some *write* them. Most also have side gigs and are there to practice skills in a safe space and to make friends without the pressure of having to be perfect, because we all are *A-Okay* with being authentic!

The Community membership is free, and if you enter the group through the URL below, you will be granted a free $29 evaluation of your Origin or Signature story (up to 10 minutes) with the purchase of this book. Either way, we're excited to see you and hear your stories!

We hope to see you there! → SellingWithYourStory.com

Acknowledgments

This book is dedicated to the brave, resilient, and often misunderstood professionals who show up every day in the network marketing space, sometimes with shaky confidence, sometimes with bold energy, but always with heart.

To the men and women building their empires from living rooms, lunch breaks, and carpool lines: you are the reason this book exists. Your commitment to doing business differently, with integrity and connection, is the spark behind every story shared here.

To my family, thank you for enduring my voice memos, note piles, and middle-of-the-night epiphanies with grace. You've witnessed every phase of this journey and never once told me to tone it down.

To the mentors and teammates who believed in this concept before it even had a name, your feedback and encouragement pushed this vision into reality. You are proof that collaboration trumps competition every single time.

To the BS Community and every reader of Selling with Stories who asked for the next level—this is it. You challenged me to go deeper, get clearer, and speak more directly to the unique challenges (and magic) of MLM leadership. I listened. And I wrote this for you.

And to anyone who still thinks "network marketers can't write real books" … thanks for the motivation.

Let this be proof: your story can sell without selling out. And your voice is more powerful than you think.

—Sydney Brown

About the Author

Sydney Brown is a business mentor, speaker, and storyteller who specializes in helping professionals harness the power of storytelling to achieve greater success. With a background in sales, coaching, and entrepreneurship, Sydney has helped countless individuals transform their communication strategies to connect with their audiences on a deeper level.

Connect with Sydney over on Facebook at RunWithSyd
https://www.facebook.com/RunWithSyd

Follow Sydney's Author Page

If you found value in this book, I would love to hear your thoughts! Leave a review on Amazon at

And follow my author page at
amazon.com/author/justsydneybrown

You can find me on most socials at GoWithSyd, RunWithSyd, or JustSydneyBrown

Your feedback helps other storytellers find their voice and their audience. Thank you for your support!

www.ingramcontent.com/pod-product-compliance
Lightning Source LLC
Chambersburg PA
CBHW070046100426
42740CB00013B/2814